018

A gift for _____

From _____

The
WILDERNESS
of GRIEF

Also by Alan Wolfelt:

Healing Your Grieving Heart: 100 Practical Ideas

*Healing A Friend's Grieving Heart: 100 Practical Ideas for
Helping Someone You Love Through Loss*

The Journey Through Grief: Reflections on Healing

*Understanding Your Grief: Ten Essential Touchstones for
Finding Hope and Healing Your Heart*

*The Understanding Your Grief Journal:
Exploring the Ten Essential Touchstones*

Companion
P R E S S

Companion Press is dedicated to the education and support of both the
bereaved and bereavement caregivers. We believe that those who companion
the bereaved by walking with them as they journey in grief have a wondrous
opportunity: to help others embrace and grow through grief—and to lead
fuller, more deeply-lived lives themselves because of this important ministry.

For a complete catalog and ordering information, write or call:

Companion Press
The Center for Loss and Life Transition
3735 Broken Bow Road Fort Collins, CO 80526
(970) 226-6050
www.centerforloss.com

The WILDERNESS of GRIEF

Finding Your Way

Alan D. Wolfelt, Ph.D.

Companion
PRESS
Fort Collins, Colorado
An imprint of the Center for Loss and Life Transition

Companion Press is an imprint of the
Center for Loss and Life Transition,
3735 Broken Bow Road, Fort Collins, Colorado 80526
970-226-6050
www.centerforloss.com

Printed in the United States of America

19 18 17 16 15 14 13   5 4 3 2

ISBN: 978-1-879651-52-4

In memory of my father, Donald Wolfelt, who inspired me by living a life of service to others

Contents

Preface

As an author, educator and grief counselor I've had the privilege to meet and "walk with" thousands of mourners. They have been so very kind to have shared their grief journeys and intimate lives with me. Without them this book could not be, nor would I be who I am.

We all experience grief in our own way and on our own schedule. Our life griefs are as unique as our fingerprints. There are really no "experts" in an area populated by so much diversity. So, I do not offer you this book as an expert, but as a fellow human being who has "walked the walk."

Most of what I have come to understand about the mystery of grief and our need to authentically mourn the deaths of those who go before us is anchored in my personal losses and the losses of those of you who have taught me about your very personal journeys. For your willingness to teach me and trust me with your stories, I thank you.

I am humbled that you have been willing to allow me to open my heart to you. For you see, I am not an expert on grief; I'm a "companion" who tries to give attention to stories of love and loss. You have taught me that grief challenges our sense of identity and the very purpose of our living.

Without some touchstones along the path, we can easily find ourselves lost in the wilderness of our grief. Our sense of connection to the world around us can seem to disappear. So, I offer you this little book to give you some hope for healing.

If, after reading this book, you're interested in learning more about the ten touchstones and perhaps jotting down your thoughts in a companion grief journal, please visit my website (www.centerforloss.com) and take a look at *Understanding Your Grief: Ten Essential Touchstones for Finding Hope and Healing Your Heart* and *The Understanding Your Grief Journal: Exploring the Ten Essential Touchstones.* Both will take you further in your exploration of the ten touchstones.

Yes, to experience and befriend the pain of loss is just as much a part of life as to experience the joy of love. That is probably why I have never met anyone mourning the death of someone precious who doesn't want to continue loving that person in some way, shape, or form.

As it should be, thoughts, feelings and behaviors that result from a death are impossible to ignore. Our experiences of grief are very powerful and demand our attention as we explore our "special needs." As we encounter loss in our lives, we have the opportunity to make a willful choice about how we are going to use the pain of grief—whether we are going to channel it to make our lives better or worse.

May the touchstones explored in this book inform your heart and comfort your spirit. May your grief be slowly and patiently transformed and your natural compassion benefit your fellow human beings and the entire world. May you find this little book to be a good companion in your journey. That is my prayer for you.

Alan D. Wolfelt

Introduction

You are grieving the death of someone you love.

Think of your grief as a wilderness—a vast, mountainous, inhospitable forest. You are in the wilderness now. You are in the midst of unfamiliar and often brutal surroundings. You are cold and tired. Yet you must journey through this wilderness. To find your way out, you must become acquainted with its terrain and learn to follow the sometimes hard-to-find trail that leads to healing.

In the wilderness of your grief, the ten touchstones explored in this book are your trail markers. They are the signs that let you know you are on the right path.

When you learn to identify and rely on the touchstones, you will not get lost in your journey, even though the trail will often be arduous and you may at times feel hopeless.

At the beginning of each touchstone you will find photos I took on a recent hiking weekend in Colorado. You might use these photos to help yourself visualize the path through the wilderness of your grief and the touchstones that will show you the way.

And even when you've become a master journeyer, and you know well the terrain of your grief, you will at times feel like you are backtracking and being ravaged by the forces around you. This, too, is the nature of grief. Complete mastery of a wilderness is not possible. Just as we cannot control the winds and the storms and the beasts in nature, we can never have total dominion over our grief.

But, if you do your work of mourning, if you become an intrepid traveler on your journey, if you make friends with these ten touchstones, I promise you that you will find your way out of the wilderness of your grief and you will learn to make the most of the rest of your precious life.

Open to the Presence
of Your Loss

It's as if the realness of what has happened
waits around a corner. I don't want to
make the turn, yet I know I must. Slowly,
I gather the courage to approach.

Someone you love has died.

In your heart, you have come to know your deepest pain. I have learned that we cannot go around the pain that is the wilderness of our grief. Instead, we must journey all through it, sometimes shuffling along the less strenuous side paths, sometimes plowing directly into the dark center.

In your willingness to embrace the pain, you honor it. Crazy as it may sound, your pain is the key that opens your heart and ushers you on your way to healing.

In many ways, and as strange as it may seem, this book is intended to help you honor your pain. Honoring means recognizing the value of and respecting. To honor your grief is not self-destructive or harmful, it is self-sustaining and life-giving!

You will learn over time that the pain of your grief will keep trying to get your attention until you have the courage to gently, and in small doses, open to its presence. The alternative—denying or suppressing your pain—is in fact more painful.

Setting your intention to heal

It takes a true commitment to heal in your grief. Yes, you are changed, but with commitment and intention you can and will become whole again. Intention is defined as being conscious of what you want to experience.

When you set your intention to heal, you commit to positively influence the course of your journey. You might tell yourself, "I can and will reach out for support in my grief. I will become filled with hope that I can and will survive this loss." Together with these words, you might form mental pictures of hugging and talking to your friends and seeing your happier self in the future.

Of course, you must still honor and embrace your pain during this time. You are committing to paying attention to your anguish in ways that allow you to begin to breathe life into your soul again.

In this book I will attempt to teach you to gently and lovingly befriend your grief. Slowly, and in "doses," you can and will return to life and begin to live again in ways that put the stars back into your sky.

Making grief your friend

To lessen your hurt, you must embrace it. As strange as it may seem, you must make it your friend.

When I reflect on making grief my friend, I think about my father. Sometimes when I fully acknowledge that I'll never see my father physically on this earth again, I am engulfed by overwhelming sadness. Then, with intention, I realize that while my father has been dead for over three years, my love for him has continued to grow. My intention is to honor his presence while acknowledging his absence. The beauty of this is that while I mourn, I can continue to love.

"Doing well" with your grief

Shame can be described as the feeling that something you are doing is bad. And you may feel that if you mourn, you should be ashamed. If you are perceived as "doing well" with your grief, you are considered "strong" and "under control."

Society also implies that if you openly express your feelings of grief, you are immature. If your feelings are fairly intense, you may be labeled "overly-emotional." If your feelings are extremely intense, you may even be referred to as "crazy."

As a professional grief counselor, I assure you that you are not immature, overly emotional, or crazy. But the societal messages surrounding grief that you may receive are!

When your personal feelings of grief are met with shame-based messages, discovering how to heal yourself becomes more difficult. If you internalize these messages, you may even become tempted to act as if you feel better than you really do. Ultimately, however, if you deny the emotions of your heart, you deny the essence of your life.

I invite you to gently confront the pain of your grief. I will show you how to look for the touchstones on your journey through the wilderness of grief so that your life can proceed with meaning and purpose.

Dispel the Misconceptions About Grief

The essence of finding meaning in the future is not to forget my past, as I have been told, but instead to embrace my past. For it is in listening to the music of the past that I can sing in the present and dance into the future.

As you journey through the wilderness of your grief, you will come to find a path that feels right for you, that is your path to healing. But beware—others will try to pull you off this path. They will try to make you believe that the path you have chosen is wrong and that their way is better.

The reason that people try to pull you off the path to healing is that they have internalized some common misconceptions about grief and mourning. And the misconceptions, in essence, deny you your right to hurt and authentically express your grief.

Misconception: Grief and mourning are the same thing.

Perhaps you have noticed that people tend to use the words "grieving" and "mourning" interchangeably. There is an important distinction, however. We move toward integrating loss into our lives not just by grieving, but by mourning.

Grief is our internal thoughts and feelings when someone we love dies.

Mourning is when you take the grief you have on the inside and express it outside of yourself. Talking about the person who died, crying, expressing your thoughts and feelings through art or music and acknowledging special anniversary dates of the person's life and death are just a few examples of mourning.

Expressing your grief outside of yourself is your way out of the wilderness. Over time and with the support of others, to mourn is to heal.

Misconception: Grief and mourning progress in predictable, orderly stages.

Probably you have already heard about the "stages of grief."

The concept of "stages" was popularized in 1969 in Elisabeth Kübler-Ross's landmark text, *On Death and Dying*. In this important book, Dr. Kübler-Ross lists the five stages of grief that she saw terminally ill patients experience in the face of their own impending deaths: denial; anger; bargaining; depression; and acceptance.

However, Kübler-Ross never intended for her stages to be interpreted as a rigid, linear sequence to be followed by all mourners.

As a grieving person, you will probably encounter others who believe that you should experience these or other "stages" in your grief journey. You may also have internalized this misconception.

Remember—do not try to determine where you "should" be in your grief journey. Just allow yourself to be naturally where you are in the process.

Everyone mourns in different ways. Personal experience is your best teacher about where you are in your unique grief journey. Don't think your goal is to move through prescribed stages of grief.

Misconception: When someone you love dies, you only grieve and mourn for the physical loss of the person.

When someone you love dies, you don't just lose the presence of that person. As a result of the death, you may lose many other connections to yourself and the world around you.

Sometimes I outline these potential losses, or what we call "secondary losses," as follows:

Loss of self

- self ("I feel like part of me died when he died.")
- identity (You may have to rethink your role as husband or wife, mother or father, son or daughter, best friend, etc.)
- self-confidence (Some grievers experience lowered self-esteem. Naturally, you may have lost one of the people in your life who gave you confidence.)
- health (Physical symptoms of mourning)
- personality ("I just don't feel like myself...")

Loss of security

- emotional security (Emotional source of support is now gone, causing emotional upheaval.)
- physical security (You may not feel as safe living in your home as you did before.)
- fiscal security (You may have financial concerns or have to learn to manage finances in ways you didn't before.)
- lifestyle (Your lifestyle doesn't feel the same as it did

before.)

Loss of meaning
- goals and dreams (Hopes and dreams for the future can be shattered.)
  - faith (You may question your faith.)
- will/desire to live (You may have questions related to future meaning in your life. You may ask, "Why go on....?")
- joy (Life's most precious emotion, happiness, is naturally compromised by the death of someone we love.)

Allowing yourself to acknowledge the many levels of loss the death has brought to your life will help you continue to "stay open" to your unique grief journey.

Misconception: After someone you love dies, the goal should be to "get over" your grief as soon as possible.

You may already have heard the question, "Are you over it yet?" Or, even worse, "Well, you should be over it by now!" To think that as a human being you "get over" your grief is ludicrous! You don't get over it, you learn to live with it. You learn to integrate the death into your life and the fabric of your being.

Misconception: Nobody can help you with your grief.

We have all heard people say, "Nobody can help you but yourself." Yet, in reality, perhaps the most compassionate thing you can do for yourself at this difficult time is to reach out to others for help.

Sharing your pain with others won't make it disappear, but it will, over time, make it more bearable. By definition, mourning requires that you get support from sources outside of yourself. Reaching out for help also connects you to other people and strengthens the bonds of love that make life seem worth living again.

Misconception: When grief and mourning are finally reconciled, they never come up again.

Oh, if only this were so. As your experience has probably already taught you, grief comes in and out like waves from the ocean. Sometimes when you least expect it, a huge wave comes along and pulls your feet right out from under you.

You will always, for the rest of your life, feel some grief over this death. It will no longer dominate your life, but it will always be there, in the background, reminding you of the love you had for the person who died.

Now that we've reviewed the common misconceptions of grief, let's wrap up Touchstone Two by listing some of the "conceptions." These are some realities you can hold onto as you journey toward healing.

Realistic expectations for grief and mourning

- You will naturally grieve, but you will probably have to make a conscious effort to mourn.
- Your grief and mourning will involve a wide variety of different thoughts and feelings.
- Your grief and mourning will impact you in all five realms of experience: physically; emotionally; cognitively ; socially; and spiritually.
- You need to feel it to heal it.
- Your grief will probably hurt more before it hurts less.
- Your grief will be unpredictable and will not likely progress in an orderly fashion.
- You don't "get over" grief; you learn to live with it.

- You need other people to help you through your grief.
- You will not always feel this bad.

Embrace the Uniqueness of Your Grief

The grief within me has its own heartbeat.
It has its own life, its own song. Part
of me wants to resist the rhythms of my
grief. Yet, as I surrender to the song, I
learn to listen deep within myself.

Let the life of this journey be just what
it is—confusing, complicated, at times
overwhelming. I must keep opening and
changing through it all until I become the
unique person who has transcended the pain
and discovered self-compassion—a vulnerable
yet grounded me who chooses to live again.

The wilderness of your grief is *your* wilderness—it is a creation of your unique self, the unique person who died, and the unique circumstances of your life.

Your wilderness may be rockier or more level. Your path may be revealed in a straight line, or, more likely, it may be full of twists and turns. In your wilderness, you will encounter places that are only meaningful to you and you will experience the topography in your own way.

Be careful about comparing your experience with that of other people. Do not adopt assumptions about how long your grief should last. Just consider taking a "one-day-at-a-time" approach. Doing so allows you to mourn at your own pace.

This touchstone invites you to explore some of the unique reasons your grief is what it is.

Your relationship with the person who died

Your relationship with the person who died was different than that person's relationship with anyone else.

Often, the stronger your attachment to the person who died, the deeper your sense of loss. It only makes sense that the closer you felt to the person who died, the more torn apart you may feel after the death. However, sometimes ambivalent relationships also create difficult grief journeys. In these cases, you may be mourning the fact that your relationship was not as close and loving as you wished it could have been.

The circumstances of the death

How, why and when the person died can have a definite impact on your journey into grief.

A sudden, unexpected death obviously did not allow you any opportunity to prepare yourself for what was about to happen. But are you ever "ready" for that moment at all? After a death due to terminal illness, friends and family members often tell me that they were still, in a sense, shocked by the death.

The age of the person who died also affects your acceptance of the death. Basically, we often find our grief easier when we feel that the person who died had a chance to live a full life.

You may also be asking yourself if you could have done anything to prevent the death. What you're really feeling is a lack of control over what happened. And accepting that we have little control over the lives of those we love is a difficult thing indeed.

The people in your life

Mourning, as I have defined it in this book, requires the outside support of other human beings in order for you to heal. Without a stabilizing support system of at least one other person, the odds are that you will have difficulty in doing this work of mourning. Healing requires an environment of empathy, caring, and gentle encouragement.

Your unique personality

Whatever your unique personality, rest assured that it will be reflected in your grief. For example, if you are quiet by nature, you may express your grief quietly. If you are outgoing, you may be more expressive with your grief. How you have responded to other losses or crises in your life will likely also be consistent with how you respond to this death.

The unique personality of the person who died

Whatever you loved most about the person who died, that is what you will now likely miss the most. And paradoxically, whatever you liked least about the person who died is what may trouble you the most now. You may have always wished you could change this aspect of his personality, but now that he is gone, you know with finality that you can't.

Whatever your feelings are about the personality of the person who died, talk about them openly. The key is finding someone you can trust who will listen to you without judging.

Your cultural background

Your cultural background is an important part of how you experience and express your grief.

When I say culture, I mean the values, rules (spoken and unspoken) and traditions that guide you and your family. Often these have been handed down generation after generation and are shaped by the countries or areas of the world your family originally came from. Your cultural background is also shaped by education, political beliefs and religion. Basically, your culture is your way of being in the world.

Your religious or spiritual background

Your personal belief system can have a tremendous impact on your journey into grief. You may discover that your religious or spiritual life is deepened, renewed, or changed as a result of your loss. Or you may well find yourself questioning your beliefs as part of your work of mourning.

Mistakenly, people may think that with faith, there is no need to mourn. Having faith does not mean you do not need to mourn. It does mean having the courage to allow yourself to mourn.

Other crises or stresses in your life right now

What else is going on in your life right now? Although we often think it shouldn't, the world does keep turning after the death of someone loved. You may have too many commitments and too little time and energy to complete them.

Take steps to de-stress your life for the time being, if at all possible. Now is the time to concentrate on mourning and healing in grief.

Your physical health

How you feel physically has a significant effect on your grief. If you are tired and eating poorly, your coping skills will be diminished. If you are sick, your bodily symptoms may be as or more pressing than your emotional and spiritual ones.

TOUCHSTONE FOUR

Explore Your
Feelings of Loss

In some ways, love and grief are very much alike. They both have the power to forever change our lives. Just as I surrender to love, I must surrender to my grief.

On your journey through the wilderness of your grief, a critical trail marker to be on the watch for is Touchstone Four, which guides you in exploring your feelings of loss.

As strange as your emotions may seem, they are a true expression of where you are right now. Rather than deny or feel victimized by your feelings, I want to help you learn to recognize and learn from them.

I have worked with thousands of grieving people and they have taught me about many, many different thoughts and feelings after a death. Rest assured that whatever you are thinking and feeling, while in one sense your thoughts and feelings are completely unique to you, they are also usually a common human response to loss.

Shock, numbness, denial and disbelief

"It feels like a dream," people in early grief often say.

Thank goodness for shock, numbness and disbelief! Other words that mourners use to describe their initial grief experience are dazed and stunned. These feelings are nature's way of temporarily protecting you from the full reality of the death.

Especially in the beginning of your grief journey, your emotions need time to catch up with what your mind has been told. On one level, you know the person is dead. But on other, deeper levels, you are not yet able or willing to truly believe it.

You may find yourself hysterically crying, having angry outbursts, or even laughing or fainting. These are all normal and necessary responses that help you survive right now.

Temporarily, denial, like shock and numbness, is also a great gift. It helps you survive. However, your denial should soften over time as you mourn and as you acknowledge, slowly and in doses, that the person you loved is truly dead.

Disorganization, confusion, searching, yearning

Perhaps the most isolating and frightening part of your grief journey is the sense of disorganization, confusion, searching and yearning that often comes with the loss. These feelings frequently arise when you begin to be confronted with the reality of the death.

You may express disorganization and confusion in your inability to complete tasks. You may feel forgetful and ineffective.

You also may experience a restless searching for the person who has died. Yearning and preoccupation with memories can leave you feeling drained. You may experience a sense of the dead person's presence, and you may catch fleeting glimpses of the person across the room. You may dream about the person who died.

Other common experiences during this time include difficulties eating and sleeping.

While it may seem strange, feelings of disorganization, confusion, searching and yearning are actually steppingstones on your path toward healing.

Anxiety, panic, fear

Feelings of anxiety, panic, and fear also may be a part of your grief experience. You may ask yourself, "Am I going to be OK? Will I survive this? Will my life have any purpose without this person?" These questions are natural. Your sense of security has been threatened, so you are naturally anxious.

A variety of thoughts and situations can increase your anxiety, panic and fear. For example, you may be afraid of what the future holds or that other people in your life will die soon. You may be more aware of your own mortality, which can be scary.

While unpleasant, anxiety, panic and fear are often normal components of the grief experience. The good news is that expressing them can help make them feel more tolerable. And knowing that they are temporary may help you during this trying time.

Explosive emotions

Anger, hate, blame, terror, resentment, rage, and jealousy are explosive emotions that may be a volatile yet natural part of your grief journey. It helps to understand that all these feelings are, at bottom, a form of protest.

Explosive emotions may surface at any time when someone you have loved dies. You cry out in anguish, "How could this happen? This isn't fair! I hate this!" You may direct these emotions at the person who died, at friends and family members, at doctors, at people who haven't experienced loss, at God.

Unfortunately, our society doesn't understand how normal and necessary these feelings can be. When you're raging or terrified, others may get upset. The intensity of your own emotions may even upset you. Still, you must give yourself permission to feel whatever you feel and to express those feelings.

If explosive emotions are part of your journey (and they aren't for everyone), be aware that you have two avenues for expression—outward or inward. The outward avenue leads to healing; the inward avenue does not. Keeping your explosive emotions inside leads to low self-esteem, depression, guilt, physical complaints and sometimes even persistent thoughts of suicide.

Experiencing explosive emotions is normal. They should, however, change in intensity and duration as you do the work of mourning. Again, I want to emphasize that the key is finding someone who will help you understand what you are feeling and allows you to embrace your grief.

Guilt and regret

Guilt, regret and self-blame are common and natural feelings after the death of someone loved. You may have a case of the "if-onlys": If only I had gotten him to the doctor sooner... If only I had been with her that night... If only I hadn't said...

If you find yourself experiencing these if-onlys, be compassionate with yourself. When someone you care about dies, it's natural to think about actions you could or could not have taken to prevent the death. But of course, you are not to blame. It's simply impossible to go through life in close relationships with other people without saying or doing something you later wish you could change.

While these feelings of guilt and regret are natural, they are sometimes not logical to those around you. When you express your guilt and regret, some people may say, "Don't be silly. There was nothing you could have done." Whether you could have done something or not is beside the point. The point is that you are feeling like you could have or should have and you need to express those feelings, however illogical.

Sadness and depression

Sadness can be the most hurtful feeling on your journey through grief. We don't want to be sad. Sadness saps pleasure from our lives. Sadness makes us feel crummy.

But sadness is a natural, authentic emotion after the death of someone loved. Something precious in your life is now gone. Of course you are sad. Of course you feel deep sorrow. Allowing yourself to feel your sadness is in large part what your journey toward healing is all about. I suggest you say out loud right now, "I have every right to feel sad!"

Weeks, or often months, will pass before you are fully confronted by the depth of your sorrow. The slowly-growing nature of this awareness is good. You could not and should not try to tolerate all of your sadness at once. Your body, mind, and spirit need time working together to embrace the depth of your loss. Be patient with yourself. Surround yourself with loving people who will understand, not judge you.

Paradoxically, the only way to lessen your pain is to move toward it, not away from it. Moving toward your sadness is not easy to do. Every time you admit to feeling sad, people around you may say things like, "Oh, don't be sad" or "Get a hold of yourself" or "Just think about what you have to be thankful for." Comments like these hinder, not help, your healing. You have been emotionally, physically and spiritually injured. Now you must attend to your injury.

Occasionally, your feelings of sorrow can be overwhelming enough to be classified as "clinical depression." After all, grief and mourning share many symptoms with depression, including sleep disturbances, appetite changes, decreased energy, withdrawal, guilt, dependency, lack of concentration and a sense of loss of control. If you feel totally immobilized, please get help from understanding friends or a professional counselor. If you're unsure if you're experiencing normal grief or clinical depression, seek out help.

Relief and release

Sometimes you may feel a sense of relief and release when someone you love dies. The death may have brought relief from suffering, particularly following an illness that was long and debilitating. Your relief, then, is normal and natural. Understand, however, that your relief does not equate to a lack of love for the person who died.

When you anticipate the death of someone who is terminally ill, you begin grieving and, I hope, mourning, long before the death itself. Your grief journey actually begins when the person you love enters the transition from living to dying. When you watch someone you love endure physical pain and loss of quality of life, you begin to understand that death can bring relief.

Allowing yourself to acknowledge relief as a part of your grief experience can be a critical step in your journey through grief. Working to embrace these feelings creates the opportunity to find hope in your healing.

A final thought about the feelings you may experience

As you journey through the wilderness of your grief, over time and with the support of others you will come to experience what I like to describe as "reconciliation." When you come out on the other side of the wilderness and you are able to fully enjoy life and living again, you have achieved reconciliation of your grief. You will learn more about this important concept in Touchstone Nine. But before we get there, let's explore some of the other trail markers to watch for on your path to healing.

Recognize You
Are Not Crazy

Grief creates a natural disorientation—a kind of emotional and spiritual wilderness.

In loss comes a period of emptiness, aloneness—new life has not yet emerged. As I commit myself to find healing, I am led to a deeper understanding of myself and a longing to return to the world around me.

In all my years as a grief counselor, the most common question mourners have asked me is, "Am I going crazy?" The second most common question is, "Am I normal?"

The journey through grief can be so radically different from our everyday realities that sometimes it feels more like being picked up and dropped onto the surface of the moon than it does a trek through the wilderness. The terrain is so very foreign and disorienting, and our behaviors in that terrain seem so out of whack, that we feel like we're going crazy.

This touchstone helps you be on the lookout for the trail marker that affirms your sanity: Recognize You Are Not Crazy. It's an important trail marker, because if you miss it, your entire journey through the wilderness of your grief may feel like Alice's surreal visit to Wonderland. (Actually, your journey may still feel surreal even if you find this trail marker, but at least you'll know in your head that you're not going crazy.)

Following are a number of common thoughts and feelings in grief that cause mourners to feel like they're going crazy. They may or may not be a part of your personal experience.

Time distortion

"I don't know what day it is, let alone what time it is!" This kind of comment is not unusual when you are mourning. Sometimes, time moves so quickly; at other times, it crawls. Your sense of past and future also may seem to be frozen in place. You may lose track of what day or even what month it is. Your inability to keep time right now isn't crazy. It's common in grief, particularly in the early days and weeks after the death.

Self-focus

Especially early in your grief, you may find yourself being less conscious of the needs of others. You may not want to listen to other people's problems. You may not have the energy to attend to all the needs of your children or other family members. You may feel flabbergasted that the world is still turning while your life is at a complete standstill.

The compulsion to focus only on your own thoughts and feelings doesn't mean you're going crazy. What it does mean is that you need to focus on yourself right now.

Re-thinking and re-telling the story

Often when someone loved dies, you find yourself thinking about the circumstances of the death and the time immediately surrounding the death over and over again. You may also feel the need—almost a compulsion—to tell other people about these prominent memories over and over again.

I call this process "telling the story." Telling the story isn't a sign that you're going crazy; in fact, it's a sign that you're doing your work of mourning. Whether you're conscious of this fact or not, you tell yourself the story and you tell others the story in an effort to integrate it into your life.

Yes, it hurts to constantly think and talk about the person you loved so much. But remember—all grief wounds get worse before they get better. Be compassionate with yourself. Try to surround yourself with people who allow and encourage you to repeat whatever you need to repeat.

Sudden changes in mood

When someone loved dies, you may feel like you are surviving fairly well one minute and in the depths of despair the next. Mood changes can make you feel like you're going crazy because you may expect yourself to keep feeling better and better. In reality, grief twists and turns like a mountainous trail. One minute you might be feeling great and the next lousy.

If you have these ups and down, don't be hard on yourself. Be patient with yourself. As you do the work of mourning and move toward healing, the periods of hopelessness will be replaced by periods of hopefulness.

Powerlessness and helplessness

Your grief can at times leave you feeling powerless. You may think or say, "What am I going to do? I feel so completely helpless." While part of you realizes you had no control over what happened, another part feels a sense of powerlessness at not having been able to prevent it. You would like to have your life back the way it was, but you can't.

Almost paradoxically, by acknowledging and allowing for temporary feelings of helplessness, you help yourself. Share your feelings with caring people around you. Remember—shared grief is diminished grief; find someone to talk to who will listen without judging.

Grief attacks or griefbursts

"I was just sailing along feeling pretty good, when out of nowhere came this overwhelming feeling of grief!" I call this a "griefburst," which is a sudden, sharp feeling of grief that can cause anxiety and pain. Some people call them grief attacks, because they attack you without warning.

During a griefburst, you may feel an overwhelming sense of missing the person you loved and find yourself openly crying, or perhaps even sobbing.

Griefbursts may feel like "crazybursts," but they are normal. When and if one strikes you, be compassionate with yourself. You have every right to miss the person who has died and to feel temporary paralysis or loss of control.

Crying and sobbing

If you're crying and sobbing a lot, you may feel like you're out of control, which can trigger your feelings of going crazy. Sobbing is an expression of the deep, strong emotions within you. These emotions need to get out, and sobbing allows for their release.

If you're crying or sobbing a lot, you're not crazy. Cry, wail and sob as long and as hard and as often as you need to.

On the other hand, if you don't cry a lot, that's OK, too. We mourn in different ways and not everyone cries. If you don't cry, it doesn't mean you aren't mourning in other ways.

Linking objects

Linking objects are items that belonged to the person who died that you now like to have around you. Objects such as clothing, books, knick-knacks, furniture, artwork, and other prized possessions can help you feel physically close to the person you miss so much.

If you like to hold, be near, look at, sleep with, caress, or even smell a special belonging of the person who died, you're not crazy. You're simply trying to hold on to a tangible, physical connection to the person.

Suicidal thoughts

Thoughts that come and go about questioning if you want to go on living can be a normal part of your grief and mourning. You might say or think, "It'd be so much easier to not be here." Usually this thought is not so much an active wish to kill yourself as it is a wish to ease your pain. Just remember that in doing the hard work of mourning, you can and will find continued meaning in life. Let yourself be helped as you have hope for your healing.

To have these thoughts is normal and not crazy; however, to make plans and take action to end your life is not normal. If thoughts of suicide take on planning and structure, get help immediately. Sometimes tunnel vision can prevent you from seeing choices. Please choose to go on living as you honor the memory of the person who died.

Dreams

Sometimes dreaming a lot about the person who died may contribute to your feelings of "going crazy." Mourners sometimes tell me that they can't stop thinking about the death—even in their sleep!

Keep in mind that dreams are one of the ways the work of mourning takes place. A dream may reflect a searching for the person who has died, for example. You may dream that you are with the person in a crowded place and lose him and cannot find him. Dreams also provide opportunities—to feel close to the person who died, to embrace the reality of the death, to gently confront the depth of the loss, to renew memories, or to develop a new self-identity. Dreams also may help you search for meaning in life and death or explore unfinished business. Finally, dreams can show you hope for the future.

On the other hand, you may experience nightmares, particularly after a traumatic, violent death. These dreams can be very frightening. If your dreams are distressing, talk about them with someone who can support and understand you.

Mystical experiences

When someone you love dies, you may have experiences that are not always rationally explainable. The primary form of mystical experience that grieving people have taught me about is communicating with the person who died.

I have listened to and learned from hundreds of people who have seen, heard, and felt the presence of someone who has died. If you count yourself among this number, you're not going crazy. You can still be very sane and exceedingly rational while at times experiencing and embracing mystical encounters. Who on this earth is to say what's real and what isn't? Certainly not I. Remain open to these experiences and be thankful for the comfort they provide.

You're not crazy, you're grieving

Never forget that your journey through the wilderness of your grief may bring you through all kinds of strange and unfamiliar terrain. As I said at the beginning of this chapter, your experiences may feel so alien that you feel more like you're on the moon! When you feel like you're going crazy, remind yourself to look for the trail marker that assures you you're not going crazy. You're grieving. The two can feel remarkably similar sometimes.

Understand the Six Needs of Mourning

I can release the pain that touches my memories, but only if I remember them. I can release my grief, but only if I express it. Memories and grief must have a heart to hold them.

If you are hoping for a map for your journey through grief, none exists. Your wilderness is an undiscovered wilderness and you its first explorer.

But virtually all mourners who have journeyed before you have found that their paths are similar. There are more commonalities than there are differences. When we are in mourning we do basically have the same needs. Instead of referring to stages of grief, I say that we as mourners have six central needs. Unlike the stages of grief you might have heard about, the six central needs of mourning are not orderly or predictable. You will probably jump around in random fashion while working on these six needs of mourning. You will address each need when you are ready to do so. Sometimes you will be working on more than one need at a time.

Mourning Need 1: Accepting the reality of the death

You can know something in your head but not in your heart. This is what often happens when someone you love dies. This first need of mourning involves gently confronting the reality that someone you care about will never physically come back into your life again.

Whether the death was sudden or anticipated, acknowledging the full reality of the loss may occur over weeks and months. You may expect him or her to come through the door, to call on the telephone, or even to touch you. To survive, you may try to push away the reality of the death at times.

One moment the reality of the loss may be tolerable; another moment it may be unbearable. Be patient with this need. As you express what you think and feel outside of yourself, you will be working on this important need.

Mourning Need 2: Letting yourself feel the pain of the loss

Like Touchstone One (open to the presence of your loss), this need of mourning requires us to embrace the pain of our loss—something we naturally don't want to do. It is easier to avoid, repress or deny the pain of grief than it is to confront it, yet it is in confronting our pain that we learn to reconcile ourselves to it.

You will probably discover that you need to dose yourself in embracing your pain. In other words, you cannot (nor should you try to) overload yourself with the hurt all at one time. Sometimes you may need to distract yourself from the pain of death, while at other times you will need to create a safe place to move toward it.

As you encounter your pain, you will also need to nurture yourself physically, emotionally and spiritually. Find others with whom you can share your painful thoughts and feelings; friends who listen without judging are your most important helpers as you work on this mourning need.

Mourning Need 3: Remembering the person who died

Do you have any kind of relationship with someone after they die? Of course. You have a relationship of memory. Precious memories, dreams reflecting the significance of the relationship and objects that link you to the person who died are examples of some of the things that give testimony to a different form of a continued relationship.

This need of mourning involves allowing and encouraging yourself to pursue this relationship.

Embracing your memories can be a very slow and, at times, painful process that occurs in small steps. Remember—don't try to do all of your work of mourning at once. Go slowly and be patient with yourself.

Following are a few example of things you can do to keep memories alive while embracing the reality that the person has died:

• Talking out or writing out favorite memories
• Giving yourself permission to keep some special keepsakes or "linking objects"
• Displaying photos of the person who died
• Visiting places of special significance that stimulate memories of times shared together
• Reviewing photo albums at special times such as holidays, birthdays, and anniversaries

In my experience, remembering the past makes hoping for the future possible. Your future will become open to new experiences only to the extent that you embrace the past.

Mourning Need 4: Developing a new self-identity

Part of your self-identity comes from the relationships you have with other people. When someone with whom you have a relationship dies, your self-identity, or the way you see yourself, naturally changes.

The way you define yourself and the way society defines you is changed. As one woman said, "I used to have a husband and was part of a couple. Now I'm not only single, but a single parent and a widow. . . I hate that word."

A death often requires you to take on new roles that had been filled by the person who died. This can be very hard work and, at times, can leave you feeling very drained of emotional, physical and spiritual energy.

Remember—do what you need to do in order to survive, for now, as you try to re-anchor yourself. To be dependent on others as you struggle with a changed identity does not make you bad or inferior. Your self-identity has been assaulted. Be compassionate with yourself. Accept the support of others.

Mourning Need 5: Searching for meaning

When someone you love dies, you naturally question the meaning and purpose of life. You probably will question your philosophy of life and explore religious and spiritual values as you work on this need. "How could God let this happen?" "Why did this happen now, in this way?"

The person who died was a part of you. This death means you mourn a loss not only outside of yourself, but inside of yourself as well. You may feel that when this person died, part of you died with him or her.

This death calls for you to confront your own spirituality. You may doubt your faith and have spiritual conflicts and questions racing through your head and heart. This is normal and part of your journey toward renewed living.

Early in your grief, allow yourself to openly mourn without pressuring yourself to have answers to such profound "meaning of life" questions. Move at your own pace as you recognize that allowing yourself to hurt and finding meaning are not mutually exclusive. More often your need to mourn and find meaning in your continued living will blend into each other, with the former giving way to the latter as healing unfolds.

Mourning Need 6: Receiving ongoing support from others

The quality and quantity of understanding support you get during your work of mourning will have a major influence on your capacity to heal. You cannot—nor should you try to—do this alone. Drawing on the experiences and encouragement of friends, fellow grievers or professional counselors is not a weakness but a healthy human need. And because mourning is a process that takes place over time, this support must be available months and even years after the death of someone in your life.

To be truly helpful, the people in your support system must appreciate the impact this death has had on you. They must understand that in order to heal, you must be allowed—even encouraged—to mourn long after the death.

You will probably discover, if you haven't already, that you can benefit from a connectedness that comes from people who also have had a death in their lives. Support groups, where people come together and share the "common bond" of experience, can be invaluable in helping you and your grief and supporting your need to mourn long after the event of the death.

Nurture Yourself

*Taking time to turn inward and slow
down helps me move from head to
heart—a realization that is necessary,
yet painful. Taking slow, deep breaths, I
encourage my body to go into neutral.*

I remind you that the word "bereaved" means "to be torn apart" and "to have special needs." Perhaps your most important "special need" right now is to be compassionate with yourself. In fact, the word "compassion" means "with passion." Caring for and about yourself with passion is self-compassion.

This touchstone is a gentle reminder to be kind to yourself as you journey through the wilderness of your grief. If you were embarking on a hike of many days through the rugged mountains of Colorado, would you dress scantily, carry little water, and push yourself until you dropped? Of course not. You would prepare carefully and proceed cautiously. You would take care of yourself because if you didn't, you could die. The consequences of not taking care of yourself in grief can be equally devastating.

Over many years of walking with people in grief, I have discovered that most of us are hard on ourselves when we are in mourning. We judge ourselves and we shame ourselves and we take care of ourselves last. But good self-care is essential to your survival. To practice good self-care doesn't mean you are feeling sorry for yourself, or being self-indulgent; rather, it means you are creating conditions that allow you to integrate the death of someone loved into your heart and soul.

I believe that in nurturing ourselves, in allowing ourselves the time and loving attention we need to journey safely and deeply through grief, we find meaning in our continued living.

Remember—self-care fortifies you for your long and challenging grief journey, a journey which leaves you profoundly affected and deeply changed. To be self-nurturing is to have the courage to pay attention to your needs.

Nurturing yourself in five important realms

When we are "torn apart," one of our most important special needs is to nurture ourselves in five important areas: physically, emotionally, cognitively, socially and spiritually.

The physical realm

Your body may be letting you know it feels distressed. Actually, one literal definition of the word "grievous" is "causing physical suffering." You may be shocked by how much your body responds to the impact of your loss.

Among the most common physical responses to loss are troubles with sleeping and low energy. You may have difficulty getting to sleep. Perhaps even more commonly, you may wake up early in the morning and have trouble getting back to sleep. During your grief journey, your body needs more rest than usual. You may also find yourself getting tired more quickly—sometimes even at the start of the day.

Muscle aches and pains, shortness of breath, feelings of emptiness in your stomach, tightness in your throat or chest, digestive problems, sensitivity to noise, heart palpitations, queasiness, nausea, headaches, increased allergic reactions, changes in appetite, weight loss or gain, agitation, and generalized tension—these are all ways your body may react to the loss of someone loved.

If you have a chronic existing health problem, it may become worse. The stress of grief can suppress your immune system and make you more susceptible to physical problems.

Good self-care is important at this time. Your body is the house you live in. Just as your house requires care and maintenance to protect you from the outside elements, your body requires that you honor it and treat it with respect. The "lethargy of grief" you are probably experiencing is a natural mechanism intended to slow you down and encourage you to care for your body.

And be certain to "talk out" your grief. Many grieving people have taught me that if they avoid or repress talking about the death, their bodies will begin to express their grief for them.

The emotional realm

We explored in Touchstone Four a number of emotions that are often part of grief and mourning. These emotions reflect that you have special needs that require support from both outside yourself and inside yourself. Becoming familiar with the terrain of these emotions can and will help you authentically mourn and heal in small doses over time. The important thing to remember is that we honor our emotions when we give attention to them.

The cognitive realm

Your mind is the intellectual ability to think, to absorb information, make decisions and reason logically. Just as your body and emotions let you know you have experienced being "torn apart," your mind has also, in effect, been torn apart.

Don't be surprised if you struggle with short-term memory problems, have trouble making even simple decisions, and think you may be "going crazy." Essentially, your mind is in a state of disorientation and confusion.

Early in your grief, you may find it helpful to allow yourself to "suspend" all thought and purposefulness for a time. Allow yourself just to be. Your mind needs time to catch up with and process your new reality.

The social realm

The death of someone you love has resulted in a very real disconnection from the world around you. When you reach out and connect with your family and friends, you are beginning to reconnect. Your link to family, friends, and community is vital for your sense of well-being and belonging.

If you don't nurture the warm, loving relationships that still exist in your life, you will probably continue to feel disconnected and isolated. You may even withdraw into your own small world and grieve, but not mourn. Isolation can then become the barrier that keeps your grief from softening over time. Allow your friends and family to nurture you. Let them in and rejoice in the connection.

The spiritual realm

When you are "torn apart," you may have many spiritual questions for which there are no easy answers: Is there a God? Why me? Will life ever be worth living again? That is why, if I could, I would encourage all of us when we are in the midst of grief to put down "Nurture my spirit" first on our daily to-do lists.

I recognize that, for some, contemplating a spiritual life in the midst of the pain of grief can be difficult. Yet, life is a miracle and we need to remind ourselves of that, during both happy times and sad times.

If you have doubt about your capacity to connect with God and the world around you, try to approach the world with the openness of a child. Embrace the pleasure that comes from the simple sights, smells, and sounds that greet your senses. You can and will find yourself rediscovering the essentials within your soul and the spirit of the world around you.

Reach Out for Help

I need not instinctively know what to do or how to be with my grief. I can reach out to others who have walked this path before. I learn that to ultimately heal, I must touch and be touched by the experiences of those who have gone before me. These people can offer me hope, inner strength and the gift of love.

When someone you love dies, you must mourn if you are to renew your capacity for love. In other words, mourning brings healing. But healing also requires the support and understanding of those around you as you embrace the pain of your loss.

I've said that the wilderness of your grief is your wilderness and that it's up to you to find your way through it. That's true. But paradoxically, you also need companionship from time to time as you journey.

Seek out the support of the people in your life who are naturally good helpers. A few solid shoulders to cry on and a handful of pairs of listening ears can make all the difference in the world. For something so difficult, it's fundamentally simple, really, this journey to healing.

Sharing your pain with others won't make it disappear, but it will, over time, make it more bearable. Reaching out for help also connects you to other people and strengthens the bonds of love that make life seem worth living again.

Where to turn for help

"There is strength in numbers," one saying goes. As you experience your grief, you may indeed find strength and a sense of stability if you draw on an entire support system for help.

Friends and family members can often form the core of your support system. Seek out people who encourage you to be yourself and who acknowledge your many thoughts and feelings about the death. What you need most now are caring, non-judgmental listeners.

You may also find comfort in talking to a clergyperson or other spiritual leader. When someone loved dies, it is natural for you to feel ambivalent about your faith and question the very meaning of life. A clergy member who responds not with criticism but with empathy to all your feelings can be a valuable resource.

A professional counselor may also be a very helpful addition to your support system. In fact, a good counselor can be something friends and family members often can't: an objective listener. A counselor's office can be that safe haven where you can reveal those feelings you're afraid to express elsewhere. What's more, a good counselor will then help you constructively channel those emotions.

For many grieving people, support groups are one of the best helping resources. In a group, you can connect with others who have experienced similar thoughts and feelings. You will be allowed and gently encouraged to talk about the person who died as much and as often as you like.

Remember, help comes in different forms for different people. The trick is to find the combination that works best for you and then make use of it.

The rule of thirds

In my own grief journeys and in the lives of the mourners I have been privileged to counsel, I have discovered that, in general, you can take all the people in your life and divide them into thirds when it comes to grief support.

One third of the people in your life will turn out to be truly empathetic helpers. They will have a desire to understand you and your unique thoughts and feelings about the death. They will demonstrate a willingness to be taught by you and a recognition that you are the expert of your experience, not them. They will be willing to be involved in your pain and suffering without feeling the need to take it away from you. They will believe in your capacity to heal.

Another third of the people in your life will turn out to be neutral in response to your grief. They will neither help nor hinder you in your journey.

And the final third of people in your life will turn out to be harmful to you in your efforts to mourn and heal. While they are usually not setting out intentionally to harm you, they will judge you, they will try to take your grief away from you, and they will pull you off the path to healing.

Seek out your friends and family members who fall into the first group. They will be your confidants and momentum-givers on your journey. When you are actively mourning, try to avoid the last group, for they will trip you up and cause you to fall.

How others can help you:
Three essentials

While there are a multitude of ways that people who care about you might reach out to help you, here are three important and fundamental helping goals. Effective helpers will help you:

1. Embrace hope.
   These are the people around you who help you sustain the presence of hope as you feel separated from those things that make life worth living. They can be present to you in your loss, yet bring you a sense of trust in yourself that you can and will heal.
2. Encounter the presence of your loss.
   These are the people who understand the need for you to revisit and recount the pain of your loss. They help you "tell your story" and provide a safe place for you to openly mourn.
3. Have "companions" in your journey.
   These people serve as companions through whom your suffering can be affirmed. They are able to break through their separation from you and truly companion

you where you are at this moment in time. They know that real compassion comes out of "walking with" you, not ahead of you or behind you.

Seek Reconciliation, Not Resolution

My grief journey has no one destination. I will not "get over it." The understanding that I don't have to be done is liberating. I will mourn this death for the rest of my life.

How do you ever find your way out of the wilderness of your grief? You don't have to dwell there forever, do you?

The good news is that no, you don't have to dwell there forever. If you follow the trail markers on your journey through the wilderness, you will find your way out. But just as with any significant experience in your life, the wilderness will always live inside you and be a part of who you are.

A number of psychological models describing grief refer to "resolution," "recovery," "reestablishment," or "reorganization" as being the destination of your grief journey.

You may have heard—indeed you may believe—that your grief journey's end will come when you resolve, or recover from, your grief.

But you may also be coming to understand one of the fundamental truths of grief: Your journey will never truly end. People do not "get over" grief. My personal and professional experience tells me that a total return to "normalcy" after the death of someone loved is not possible; we are all forever changed by the experience of grief.

Reconciliation is a term I find more appropriate for what occurs as you work to integrate the new reality of moving forward in life without the physical presence of the person who died. With reconciliation comes a renewed sense of energy and confidence, an ability to fully acknowledge the reality of the death and a capacity to become re-involved in the activities of living. There is also an acknowledgment that pain and grief are difficult, yet necessary, parts of life.

As the experience of reconciliation unfolds, you will recognize that life is and will continue to be different without the presence of the person who died. Changing the relationship with the person who died from one of presence to one of memory and redirecting one's energy and initiative toward the future often takes longer—and involves more hard work—than most people are aware. We, as human beings, never resolve our grief, but instead become reconciled to it.

We come to reconciliation in our grief journeys when the full reality of the death becomes a part of us. Beyond an intellectual working through of the death, there is also an emotional and spiritual working through. What had been understood at the "head" level is now understood at the "heart" level.

You will find that as you achieve reconciliation, the sharp, ever-present pain of grief will give rise to a renewed sense of meaning and purpose. Your feelings of loss will not completely disappear, yet they will soften, and the intense pangs of grief will become less frequent. Hope for a continued life will emerge as you are able to make commitments to the future, realizing that the person you have given love to and received love from will never be forgotten. The unfolding of this journey is not intended to create a return to an "old normal" but the discovery of a "new normal."

Reconciliation emerges much in the way grass grows. Usually we don't check our lawns daily to see if the grass is growing, but it does grow and soon we come to realize it's time to mow the grass again. Likewise, we don't look at ourselves each day as mourners to see how we are healing. Yet we do come to realize, over the course of months and years, that we have come a long way. We have taken some important steps toward reconciliation.

Usually there is not one great moment of "arrival," but subtle changes and small advancements. It's helpful to have gratitude for even very small advancements, If you are beginning to taste your food again, be thankful. If you mustered the energy to meet your friend for lunch, be grateful. If you finally got a good night's sleep, rejoice.

Of course, you will take some steps backward from time to time, but that is to be expected. Keep believing in yourself. Set your intention to reconcile your grief and have hope that you can and will come to live and love again.

Signs of reconciliation

How do you know if you are moving toward reconciling your loss? Here are some signs to look for that let you know that you are making progress in your journey through the wilderness of grief.

- A recognition of the reality and finality of the death
- A return to stable eating and sleeping patterns
- A renewed sense of release from the person who has died. You will have thoughts about the person, but you will not be preoccupied by these thoughts.

- The capacity to enjoy experiences in life that are normally enjoyable
- The establishment of new and healthy relationships
- The capacity to live a full life without feelings of guilt or lack of self-respect
- The drive to organize and plan one's life toward the future
- The serenity to become comfortable with the way things are rather than attempting to make things as they were
- The versatility to welcome more change in your life
- The awareness that you have allowed yourself to fully grieve and mourn, and you have survived
- The awareness that you do not "get over" your grief; instead, you have a new reality, meaning and purpose in your life
- The acquaintance of new parts of yourself that you have discovered in your grief journey
- The adjustment to new role changes that have resulted from the loss of the relationship
- The acknowledgment that the pain of loss is an inherent part of life resulting from the ability to give and receive love

Remember that reconciliation is an ongoing process. If you are early in your work of mourning, you may not have found any of these signs yet in your journey. Rest assured that as time passes and you do the hard work of mourning, you will recognize more and more of these signs in your daily life.

Appreciate Your Transformation

*This death has made me look at what is
important in life. How very important
are the choices I make each moment
both to myself and those I love.*

*I have discovered a new sense of direction
and purpose in my life. I have reassessed
my goals, reset my priorities and become
deeply connected to those I love.*

The journey through grief is life-changing. When you leave the wilderness of your grief, you are simply not the same person as you were when you entered the wilderness. You have been through so much. How could you be the same?

I'm certain you have discovered that you have been transformed by your journey into grief. Transformation literally means an entire change in form. Many mourners have said to me, "I have grown from this experience. I am a different person." You are indeed different now. Your inner form has changed. You have likely grown in your wisdom, in your understanding, in your compassion.

Growth means change.

We as human beings are forever changed by the death of someone in our lives. You may discover that you have developed new attitudes. You may be more patient or more sensitive to the feelings and circumstances of others, especially those suffering from loss. You may have new insights that guide the way you live your new life. You may have developed new skills. You may have learned to balance your own checkbook or cook a nice meal.

You are "new," different than you were prior to the death. To the extent that you are different, you can say you have grown.

Growth means a new inner balance with no end points.

While you may do your work of mourning in ways that help you recapture some sense of inner balance, it is a new inner balance. The word growth reflects that you do not reach some final end point in your grief journey.

None of us totally completes the mourning process. People who think you "get over" grief" are often striving to pull it together while at the same time feeling that something is missing.

You don't return to a previous "inner balance" or "normal" but instead eventually achieve a new inner balance and a new normal.

Growth means exploring your assumptions about life.

The death of someone in your life invites you to look at your assumptions about life. Your loss experiences have a tendency to transform your assumptions, values and priorities. What you may have thought of as being important—your nice house, your new car—may not matter any longer. The job or sport or financial goal that used to drive you may now seem trivial.

When someone loved dies, you may also find yourself questioning your religious and spiritual values. You might ask questions like, "How did God let this happen?" or "Why did this happen to our family?" or "Why should I get my feet out of bed?"

Exploring these questions is a long and arduous part of the grief journey. But ultimately, exploring our assumptions about life can make these assumptions richer and more life-affirming.

Growth means utilizing your potential.

The grief journey often challenges you to reconsider the importance of using your potential. In some ways, death loss seems to free the potential within. Questions such as "Who am I? What am I meant to do with my life?" often naturally arise during grief. Answering them inspires a hunt. You may find yourself searching for your very soul.

In part, seeking purpose means living inside the question, "Am I making a living doing the work I love to do?" Beyond that, it means being able to say, "Does my life really matter?" Rather than dragging you down, your grief may ultimately lift you up. Then it becomes up to you to embrace and creatively express your newfound potential.

Final thoughts on healing your heart

Tomorrow is now. It is here. It is waiting for you. You have many choices in living the transformation that grief has brought to your life.

You can choose to visualize your heart opening each and every day. When your heart is open, you are receptive to what life brings you, both happy and sad. By "staying open," you create a gateway to your healing.

When this happens you will know that the long nights of suffering in the wilderness have given way to a journey towards the dawn. You will know that new life has come as you celebrate the first rays of a new light and new beginning. Choose life!

As you continue to experience how grief has transformed you, be open to the new directions your life is now taking. You have learned to watch for trail markers in your grief. Now learn to watch for trail markers in your continued living. Listen to the wisdom of your inner voice. Make choices that are congruent with what you have learned on your journey.

Right now, take a moment to close your eyes, open your heart, and remember the smile of the person who died.

Bless you. I hope we meet one day.

The Mourner's Bill of Rights

Though you should reach out to others as you journey through grief, you should not feel obligated to accept the unhelpful responses you may receive from some people. You are the one who is grieving, and as such, you have certain "rights" no one should try to take away from you.

The following list is intended both to empower you to heal and to decide how others can and cannot help. This is not to discourage you from reaching out to others for help, but rather to assist you in distinguishing useful responses from hurtful ones.

1. *You have the right to experience your own unique grief.*
   No one else will grieve in exactly the same way you do. So, when you turn to others for help, don't allow them to tell what you should or should not be feeling.

2. *You have the right to talk about your grief.*
   Talking about your grief will help you heal. Seek out others who will allow you to talk as much as you want, as often as you want, about your grief. If at times you don't feel like talking, you also have the right to be silent.

3. *You have the right to feel a multitude of emotions.*
   Confusion, disorientation, fear, guilt and relief are
   just a few of the emotions you might feel as part of
   your grief journey. Others may try to tell you that
   feeling angry, for example, is wrong. Don't take these
   judgmental responses to heart. Instead, find listeners
   who will accept your feelings without condition.

4. *You have the right to be tolerant of your physical and
   emotional limits.*
   Your feelings of loss and sadness will probably leave
   you feeling fatigued. Respect what your body and
   mind are telling you. Get daily rest. Eat balanced
   meals. And don't allow others to push you into doing
   things you don't feel ready to do.

5. *You have the right to experience "griefbursts."*
   Sometimes, out of nowhere, a powerful surge of grief
   may overcome you. This can be frightening, but it is
   normal and natural. Find someone who understands
   and will let you talk it out.

6. *You have the right to make use of ritual.*
   The funeral ritual does more than acknowledge the
   death of someone loved. It helps provide you with

the support of caring people. More important, the
funeral is a way for you to mourn. If others tell you
the funeral or other healing rituals such as these are
silly or unnecessary, don't listen.

7. *You have the right to embrace your spirituality.*
   If faith is a part of your life, express it in ways that
   seem appropriate to you. Allow yourself to be around
   people who understand and support your religious
   beliefs. If you feel angry at God, find someone to talk
   with who won't be critical of your feelings of hurt
   and abandonment.

8. *You have the right to search for meaning.*
   You may find yourself asking, "Why did he or she die?
   Why this way? Why now?" Some of your questions
   may have answers, but some may not. And watch out
   for the clichéd responses some people may give you.
   Comments like, "It was God's will" or "Think of what
   you still have to be thankful for" are not helpful and
   you do not have to accept them.

9. *You have the right to treasure your memories.*
   Memories are one of the best legacies that exist
   after the death of someone loved. You will always

remember. Instead of ignoring your memories, find others with whom you can share them.

10. *You have the right to move toward your grief and heal.* Reconciling your grief will not happen quickly. Remember, grief is best experienced in "doses." Be patient and tolerant with yourself and avoid people who are impatient and intolerant with you. Neither you nor those around you must forget that the death of someone loved changes your life forever.

About the Author

Author, educator and grief counselor Dr. Alan Wolfelt is known across North America for his compassionate messages about healing in grief. He is committed to helping people mourn well so they can go on to live well and love well.

Dr. Wolfelt is founder and Director of the Center for Loss and Life Transition, located in the beautiful mountain foothills of Fort Collins, Colorado. Past recipient of the Association of Death Education and Counseling's Death Educator Award, he is also a faculty member of the University of Colorado Medical School's Department of Family Medicine.